AF656268

Sanjeev Kapoor

Delicious Soups

In association with Alyona Kapoor

Popular Prakashan
www.popularprakashan.com

Published by
POPULAR PRAKASHAN PVT. LTD.
301, Mahalaxmi Chambers
22, Bhulabhai Desai Road
Mumbai - 400 026
for Khana Khazana Publications Pvt. Ltd.

© 2011 Sanjeev Kapoor
First Published March 2011
Third Reprint January 2015

WORLD RIGHTS RESERVED. The contents – all recipes, photographs and drawings are original and copyrighted. No portion of this book shall be reproduced, stored in a retrieval system or transmitted by any means, electronic, mechanical, photocopying, recording or otherwise, without the written permission of the author and the publisher.

(4390)
ISBN: 978-81-7991-642-1

Design: Anjali Sawant
Photography: Alim Bolar, Mangesh Parab, Mukesh Munim, Sanjeev Nadkarni and Satish Parab

PRINTED IN INDIA
by Rama Printer
4743/23, Ansari Road, Darya Ganj
New Delhi-110002

Author's Note

We all crave a bowl of steaming soup every now and then. Soups are healthy and comforting, and they don't always have to be straight out of a tin or packet. Wouldn't it be fun to make your own steaming bowl from scratch! No added preservatives, flavour or colour, just natural ingredients and a recipe in hand! Home-made soups don't cost much, are a lot of fun to make, and a healthy choice, when you're craving a snack.

A clear soup will cleanse your palate or set the tone before a fine dining experience. However, soups are no longer just a prelude to a meal. They can easily be the main event – a thick and chunky soup, with a piece of crusty bread on the side, makes for a truly filling meal.

Stir up a quick soup on the go, or put on a pot and let it simmer till liquid gold. Throw in some leftovers - surprisingly good additions to soups - and you have a bowl of contentment that will leave you with a warm afterglow.

Find out how, with my selection of Indian and international soups. Sip on the light and refreshing Clear Lemon and Coriander Soup; slurp on delicious Creamed Red Pumpkin and Apple Soup; indulge on the creamy Mushroom Soup with Almonds; or guzzle a bowl of rustic Spinach and Rice Soup and treat your senses to some delicious soups!

Happy Cooking!

Contents

Roasted Pepper Soup

5 medium red capsicums, halved and seeded

2 medium yellow capsicums, halved and seeded

1 large onion, chopped

4 garlic cloves, crushed

1 tablespoon refined flour

5 cups Vegetable Stock (page 94)

5 fresh basil leaves

Salt to taste

1 teaspoon sugar

½ teaspoon black pepper powder

- Prick the capsicums with a fork and roast them directly on open flame on low heat till lightly charred. Plunge them into cold water, remove skin and chop them roughly.

- Place the onion and garlic in a non-stick pan and roast on medium heat for a minute. Add the refined flour and continue to roast for another minute till lightly browned or till fragrant.

Roasted Pepper Soup

- Add one cup of vegetable stock, capsicums and two to three fresh basil leaves. Stir and bring to a boil. Cover and simmer for three to four minutes. Cool and blend to a smooth purée.
- Transfer into a thick-bottomed non-stick pan, add the remaining stock and bring to a boil.
- Lower the heat, add salt, sugar and pepper powder. Simmer for two to three minutes.
- Serve hot garnished with the remaining fresh basil leaves.

Caldo Verde

30 spinach leaves, finely chopped

3 medium potatoes, boiled and mashed

1 medium onion, finely chopped

4 cups Vegetable Stock (page 94)

Salt to taste

½ teaspoon black pepper powder

½ cup milk

- Heat a deep non-stick pan. Add the onion and roast for a couple of minutes taking care that the colour of the onion does not change. Add the vegetable stock and bring it to a boil.
- Add the potatoes and mix well. Add the spinach and cook till the leaves are tender. Add salt to taste and the pepper powder.
- Add the milk and bring it to a boil.
- Remove from heat and serve piping hot.

Gajar Ki Kanji

4 large carrots, peeled and cut into thin sticks

1 large beetroot, peeled and cut into thin sticks

2 tablespoons mustard seeds, coarsely powdered

1 tablespoons salt

1½ tablespoons coarse red chilli powder

- Pour eighteen cups of water into a large jar or a clay pot (*matka*), with a capacity of five litres. Add the carrots, beetroot, powdered mustard, salt and chilli powder, and mix.
- Cover the pot with a piece of muslin and fasten it around the rim with a piece of string.

- Stand the jar in direct sunlight for three to four days. Place in a refrigerator to chill.
- Pour into tall glasses with some pieces of carrot and beetroot, and serve chilled.

Chef's Tip

Traditionally black carrots are used to make *kanji*. If using them, omit the beetroot.

Note: *Do not dilute the kanji with water to make it last longer, for both the colour and taste are lost. If it gets over, make a fresh lot.*

Carrot And Almond Soup

4 medium carrots, chopped
12-15 almonds
2 teaspoons olive oil
1 medium leek, chopped
1 medium onion, chopped
Salt to taste
¼ teaspoon black pepper powder
2 tablespoons fresh breadcrumbs

- Heat the olive oil in a large non-stick pan over medium heat. Add the carrots, leek, onion and ten to twelve almonds; cook for one minute. Cut the remaining almonds into slivers.
- Add the salt, pepper powder and fresh breadcrumbs, and mix well. Add four cups of water and boil for ten minutes.
- Strain the mixture and reserve the liquid. Purée the vegetables in a blender with chilled water, if the vegetables are too hot.
- Bring the strained liquid to a boil. Add the puréed vegetables and stir to mix well. Lower heat and simmer for five minutes. Serve piping hot, garnished with almond slivers.

Gajar Shorba With Crisp Spinach And Toasted Sesame Seeds

5 medium carrots, grated

2 cups fresh spinach leaves, shredded

4 teaspoons sesame seeds, toasted

1 tablespoon butter

1 teaspoon cumin seeds

4 garlic cloves, chopped

1 inch ginger, chopped

4 cups Vegetable Stock (page 94)

1 potato, boiled and mashed

2 teaspoons black peppercorns, crushed

Salt to taste

Oil for deep-frying

- Heat the butter in a non-stick pan; add the cumin seeds and when they begin to change colour, add the garlic, ginger and carrots.

- Add one cup of stock and cook till the carrots are soft. Remove from heat, cool and purée in a blender.

- Transfer the purée to a non-stick pan and add the mashed potato, remaining stock, crushed peppercorns and salt. Cook, stirring continuously, till the soup comes to a boil. Pass the soup through a strainer.

- For the crisp spinach, heat sufficient oil in a non-stick wok; add the spinach and deep-fry till crisp. Drain on absorbent paper.

- Pour the soup into individual bowls, garnish with the spinach and sprinkle sesame seeds on top. Serve immediately.

Gajar Shorba with Crisp Spinach and Toasted Sesame Seeds

Microwaved Fresh Tomato Soup

8 medium tomatoes, quartered

1 medium carrot, cut in round slices

1 medium onion, sliced

6 garlic cloves, chopped

2-inch celery stalk, chopped

½ tablespoon oil

1 tablespoon butter

1 bay leaf

Salt to taste

1 teaspoon sugar

4-6 black peppercorns, crushed

¼ cup cream

A few sprigs of parsley, chopped

12-16 bread croûtons (see below)

- Put the oil, butter, carrot, onion, garlic, celery, and bay leaf in a large microwave-safe bowl and cook for five minutes on HIGH (100%).
- Add the tomatoes, salt, sugar and three cups of water and cook, covered, on HIGH (100%) for twenty-five minutes.

- Leave to cool slightly. Purée the tomato mixture in a blender till smooth. Transfer the purée to a microwave-safe bowl. Add the crushed peppercorns and cook on HIGH (100%) for five minutes.
- Remove from the oven, stir in the cream and garnish with chopped parsley. Serve piping hot with bread croûtons.

Note: *To make bread croûtons, cut two bread slices into half-inch squares. Place on a microwave-safe plate and cook on HIGH (100%) for ten minutes. Alternatively, the bread slices can be grilled in a Combi-oven till crisp.*

Tomato Saar

9 medium tomatoes, roughly chopped

2 tablespoons oil

5-6 garlic cloves, chopped

2 bay leaves

15 black peppercorns

1 inch ginger, chopped

1 teaspoon mustard seeds

8-10 curry leaves

1 teaspoon cumin seeds

3-4 green chillies, slit

¼ teaspoon asafoetida

Salt to taste

1 tablespoon grated coconut

1 tablespoon chopped fresh coriander

- Heat one tablespoon of oil in a deep non-stick pan; add the garlic, bay leaves, ten peppercorns and ginger, and sauté for one minute.
- Add the tomatoes and cook for ten minutes. Add four cups of water and bring to a boil.

- Strain the mixture into a bowl. Cool the residue and purée in a blender.
- Crush the remaining peppercorns.
- Heat the remaining oil in another deep non-stick pan; add the mustard seeds, curry leaves, crushed peppercorns, cumin seeds, green chillies, asafoetida and salt, and sauté for a minute.
- Add the purée and the stock, and mix well. Bring the mixture to a boil. Add the grated coconut and chopped coriander. Serve hot.

Cream Of Vegetable Soup With Spinach

½ medium cabbage, chopped

1 medium carrot, chopped

4-5 small cauliflower florets, grated

6-8 French beans, chopped

1 medium potato, boiled and chopped

200 grams spinach, shredded

1 tablespoon butter

1 medium onion, chopped

2 teaspoons refined flour

2 cups Vegetable Stock (page 94) or water

Salt to taste

White pepper powder to taste

2 cups cream

- Heat the butter in a non-stick pan; add the onion and sauté for two minutes over medium heat.
- Add the cabbage, carrot, cauliflower and French beans. Stir and cook on high heat for three to four minutes.

Cream of Vegetable Soup with Spinach

- Sprinkle the refined flour and cook over medium heat, stirring continuously, for two minutes, or till fragrant.
- Stir in the vegetable stock or water and salt, and bring to a boil. Add the potato and white pepper powder, and cook till the vegetables are soft.
- Add the spinach and simmer for three to four minutes. If the mixture is too thick, add a little more vegetable stock and adjust the consistency.
- Add the cream and remove from the heat. Serve hot.

Creamed Red Pumpkin And Apple Soup

250 grams red pumpkin, grated
2 apples, roughly chopped
2 teaspoons oil
2 bay leaves
1 large onion, roughly chopped
1½ cups Vegetable Stock (page 94)
1 cup milk
2 teaspoons lemon juice
Salt to taste
2 teaspoons curry powder
½ teaspoon black pepper powder
A few leaves of parsley

- Heat the oil in a non-stick pan; add the bay leaves and chopped onion, and sauté till translucent.
- Add the pumpkin and apples. Cook on high heat for a couple of minutes, stirring continuously.

- Add half the stock and cook the vegetables until soft.
- Remove from heat and set aside to cool. Discard the bay leaf. Purée the cooled vegetables in a blender. Transfer the purée to a non-stick pan and heat. Stir in the remaining stock and milk, and bring to a boil.
- Add the lemon juice, salt, curry powder and pepper powder. Stir well to mix.
- Serve hot, garnished with parsley.

Mushroom Soup With Almonds

400 grams fresh button mushrooms, chopped

30 almonds

1 tablespoon butter

2 medium onions, finely chopped

5 cups milk

Salt to taste

White pepper powder to taste

- Blanch the almonds in one cup of hot water. Drain and peel; crush twenty almonds coarsely and cut the rest into thin slivers.
- Heat the butter in a non-stick pan; add the onions and mushrooms, and sauté till they soften. Cool and process in a blender to make a smooth purée.
- Transfer the purée to a non-stick pan; add the milk and mix well. Bring to a boil over medium heat. Add the crushed almonds, salt and pepper powder, and stir to mix.
- Serve piping hot, garnished with the almond slivers.

Carrot And Coriander Soup

650 grams carrots, roughly chopped

1 cup tightly-packed fresh coriander

2 tablespoons butter

2 bay leaves

1 teaspoon black peppercorns

1 medium onion, chopped

6-8 garlic cloves, chopped

½ teaspoon white pepper powder

Salt to taste

- Finely chop the fresh coriander and reserve the stems.
- Heat the butter in a non-stick pan; add the bay leaves, peppercorns, onion and garlic, and sauté for two minutes.
- Add the carrots, coriander stems and six cups of water and bring to a boil. Cook till the carrots are tender and soft.

Carrot and Coriander Soup

- Remove the carrots and coriander stems from the stock, cool and transfer to a blender to make a fine purée. Reduce the stock slightly by boiling; strain.

- Transfer the purée to a non-stick pan and add the strained stock to get the desired consistency. Bring to a boil again.

- Add the white pepper powder mixed with a little water. Add salt to taste. Stir in the chopped coriander and serve piping hot.

Hot And Sour Vegetable Soup

1 slice bamboo shoot

½ medium carrot, grated

¼ small cabbage, finely chopped

2 fresh button mushrooms, finely chopped

½ medium green capsicum, finely chopped

4-6 French beans, finely chopped

2 tablespoons oil

1 small onion, finely chopped

2-3 garlic cloves, finely chopped

1 inch ginger, grated

2-inch celery stalk, finely chopped

½ teaspoon white pepper powder

Salt to taste

½ teaspoon sugar

¼ teaspoon MSG (optional)

2 tablespoons soy sauce

2 tablespoons green chilli sauce

4-5 cups Vegetable Stock (page 94)

3 tablespoons cornflour

2 tablespoons white vinegar

1 tablespoon Chilli Oil (page 93)

1 spring onion green stalk, finely chopped

- Boil the bamboo shoot in one cup of water for two to three minutes. Drain and chop fine.
- Heat oil in a wok or non-stick pan; add the onion, garlic and ginger, and stir-fry for one minute.
- Add the bamboo shoot, carrot, cabbage, mushrooms, green capsicum, French beans and celery.
- Cook, stirring continuously, for two to three minutes, or until vegetables are almost cooked.
- Add the white pepper powder, salt to taste, sugar, MSG, soy sauce, green chilli sauce, and mix well.
- Stir in the vegetable stock and bring to a boil. Mix the cornflour with half a cup of water and stir into the soup.

- Cook, stirring continuously, for one minute or until the soup thickens.
- Stir in the vinegar, drizzle the chilli oil over and serve piping hot, garnished with chopped spring onion greens.

Chef's Tip

We have used tinned bamboo shoots which are preserved in brine, hence they have to be boiled in water before use.

Mushroom Cappuccino

15 large fresh button mushrooms, thickly sliced

2 cups milk, chilled

1 tablespoon butter

1 bay leaf

1 small onion, chopped

4-6 garlic cloves, chopped

4 cups Vegetable Stock (page 94)

Salt to taste

¼ teaspoon white pepper powder

¾ cup cream

1 teaspoon cinnamon powder

- Melt the butter in a heavy-bottomed non-stick pan. Add the bay leaf, onion and garlic, and sauté for two to three minutes or till the onion is translucent.
- Add the mushrooms and sauté for one minute. Add one cup of vegetable stock and cook for five more minutes. Remove from the heat and cool.

Mushroom Cappuccino

- Remove the bay leaf and discard.
- Make a purée of the cooked mushrooms and add the remaining vegetable stock. Return to the heat and bring to a boil. Add salt and white pepper powder, lower the heat and simmer for two to three minutes.
- Stir in the cream and remove from the heat. Pour the soup into individual cups and keep warm.
- Pour the chilled milk into a chilled bowl. Beat with a fork till it develops a thick froth. Collect the froth with a ladle and place on the hot mushroom soup giving it a cappuccino effect.
- Sprinkle cinnamon powder and serve immediately.

Chef's Tip

Use milk with a high fat content for a thick froth.

Lettuce And Cottage Cheese Broth

20 romaine lettuce leaves, roughly torn

150 grams cottage cheese, cut into ½-inch cubes

1 medium carrot, peeled and thinly sliced

2 spring onions with greens

1 inch ginger, finely chopped

1½ teaspoons refined oil

4 cups Vegetable Stock (page 94)

1 tablespoon soya sauce

2 tablespoons dry sherry

1 teaspoon sugar

Salt to taste

Black pepper powder to taste

1 teaspoon red chilli flakes

1 teaspoon vinegar

- Wash and cut the spring onion bulbs into slices. Chop the spring onion greens.
- Heat a non-stick pan and sauté the cottage cheese in a little oil on high heat until golden brown. Remove from the pan and place on absorbent paper.

- Heat the remaining oil in the same pan and sauté the sliced spring onion bulbs, carrot and ginger for half a minute.
- Add the vegetable stock and bring to a boil. Stir in the soy sauce and dry sherry, and season with sugar, salt and pepper powder. Add the cottage cheese and the lettuce, and stir gently to mix.
- Stir in the red chilli flakes and vinegar.
- Serve piping hot, garnished with spring onion greens.

Mushroom And Paneer Clear Soup

6 fresh button mushrooms, sliced

150 grams cottage cheese, grated

½ tablespoon refined flour

1 teaspoon oil + for deep-frying

2 spring onions, chopped

2 garlic cloves, chopped

4-5 cups Vegetable Stock (page 94)

Salt to taste

½ tablespoon soy sauce

¼ teaspoon MSG (optional)

1 celery stalk, chopped

8-10 black peppercorns, crushed

¼ cup blanched vermicelli

1½ teaspoons lemon juice

4-5 fresh basil leaves

- Mix the grated cottage cheese with refined flour and knead into a smooth dough. Divide into eight equal portions and shape into balls. Heat sufficient oil in a *kadai* and deep-fry till light golden. Drain on absorbent paper.

- Heat one teaspoon of oil in a wok; add the spring onions and garlic, and sauté over medium heat for half a minute. Add the mushrooms and continue to sauté for another minute.
- Add the vegetable stock and bring to a boil.
- Add the salt, soy sauce, MSG, celery and crushed peppercorns. Simmer, uncovered, for four to five minutes.
- Stir in the vermicelli, fried cottage cheese balls and lemon juice.
- Ladle immediately into individual soup bowls and serve hot, garnished with roughly torn basil leaves.

Mushroom and Paneer Clear Soup

Mixed Vegetable Soup

1 medium carrot, finely chopped

1 medium potato, finely chopped

¼ medium green cabbage, finely chopped

6-8 French beans, finely chopped

6-8 fresh button mushrooms, finely chopped

1 medium capsicum, finely chopped

4-5 small cauliflower florets

1 tablespoon oil

2 bay leaves

1 medium onion, finely chopped

2 teaspoons wholewheat flour

Salt to taste

White pepper powder to taste

2 cups Vegetable Stock (page 94) or water

2 cups milk

- Soak the chopped potato in water to avoid discolouration. Grate the cauliflower florets along with the tender part of the stem.
- Heat the oil in a thick-bottomed non-stick pan; add the bay leaves and chopped onion, and sauté for two minutes over medium heat. Drain the chopped potato and add to the pan.
- Add the carrot, mushrooms, cabbage, French beans and grated cauliflower. Stir and cook on high heat for three to four minutes.
- Sprinkle the wholewheat flour and cook, stirring continuously over medium heat, for two minutes, or till fragrant. Add the salt and white pepper powder.
- Stir in the vegetable stock and bring to a boil. Add the chopped capsicum. Lower the heat and simmer till the vegetables are cooked and the soup is fairly thick.
- Gradually stir in the milk and simmer for three to four minutes, or till it reaches the desired consistency. Remove the bay leaf, adjust the seasoning and serve piping hot.

Palak Shorba

500 grams fresh spinach leaves
2 tablespoons olive oil
3 black cardamoms
2 cloves
1 inch cinnamon
2 tablespoons refined flour
3 inches ginger, chopped
5 garlic cloves, chopped
1 medium onion, chopped
4-5 black peppercorns
4 bay leaves
Salt to taste
¼ teaspoon white pepper powder
1 teaspoon roasted cumin powder

- Blanch the spinach leaves in boiling hot water for two to three minutes. Drain, refresh in cold water and purée in a mixer.
- Heat the olive oil in a deep non-stick pan. Add the black cardamoms, cloves, cinnamon and refined flour, and sauté for two to three minutes.

- Add the ginger, garlic and onion, and sauté for about five minutes.
- Add the peppercorns, bay leaves, salt, white pepper powder, roasted cumin powder and five cups of water. Stir, lower the heat and simmer for ten minutes, stirring occasionally.
- Strain the stock. Add the spinach purée to the strained stock and mix well.
- Cook for four to five minutes. Serve piping hot.

Cabbage Soup

1 medium cabbage, diced

2 medium onions, diced

Salt to taste

4 medium tomatoes, diced

Black pepper powder to taste

2 medium green capsicums, diced

4 teaspoons lemon juice

- Heat a deep non-stick pan. Add the onions and roast for a minute.
- Add the cabbage and salt, and stir. Add four cups of water, cover and cook for two to three minutes.
- Add the tomatoes and pepper powder, and stir. Continue to cook for another two to three minutes.
- Add the capsicums, cover and cook for seven to eight minutes.
- Add the lemon juice and mix. Serve piping hot.

Cabbage Soup

Roasted Onion, Garlic And Pumpkin Soup

2 medium onions

2 whole garlic bulbs

700 grams red pumpkin, peeled and thinly sliced

3 tablespoons oil

Salt to taste

½ cup fresh cream (optional)

- Heat one and a half tablespoons of oil in a non-stick pan and add the pumpkin slices. Sprinkle some salt over them and cook on medium heat till well roasted.
- Place the whole onions and garlic bulbs, without peeling, in a microwave oven and cook on HIGH (100%) for one minute, so that they soften.
- Heat the remaining oil in another non-stick pan and roast the onions and garlic on medium heat till fragrant and the peels begin to loosen.

- Peel the garlic cloves and add to the pumpkin. Peel the onions and roughly chop them and add to the pumpkin. Add half a cup of water, cover the pan and cook on medium heat till the pumpkin is soft. Cool.

- Transfer the mixture to a blender, add one-fourth cup of water and blend to a smooth purée.

- Transfer the purée to the pan, adjust the salt and bring to a boil. Stir in the cream. Serve hot.

Dahi Shorba

1 cup yogurt

2 teaspoons gram flour

1-2 green chillies, chopped

1 inch ginger, chopped

¼ teaspoon sugar

Salt to taste

2 teaspoons ghee

1 teaspoon cumin seeds

1 medium carrot, finely chopped

4-6 French beans, finely chopped

2 tablespoons shelled green peas

1 medium green capsicum, finely chopped

5-6 small cauliflower florets, finely chopped

- Grind the green chillies and ginger to a fine paste.
- Whisk the yogurt with three cups of water. Add the gram flour, green chilli-ginger paste, sugar and salt, and mix well.

- Heat the ghee in a thick-bottomed non-stick pan; add the cumin seeds and stir-fry until light golden brown. Add the chopped carrot, beans, peas, capsicum and cauliflower, and sauté the vegetables for two or three minutes.

- Stir in the yogurt mixture and bring to a boil; lower the heat and simmer for eight to ten minutes, or until thick.

- Adjust the seasoning and serve hot.

Spinach And Rice Soup

600 grams spinach, blanched and puréed

¼ cup arborio rice, soaked

2 tablespoons olive oil

1 small onion, chopped

2 garlic cloves, chopped

1 small red chilli, seeded and chopped

6 cups Vegetable Stock (page 94)

Salt to taste

10-12 black peppercorns, freshly ground

4 tablespoons grated Parmesan cheese

- Heat the olive oil in a large non-stick pan; add the onion, garlic and chilli, and sauté for about five minutes or until softened.
- Drain the rice and add to the pan. Stir well, add the vegetable stock and bring to a boil.

Spinach and Rice Soup

- Lower the heat and simmer for another ten minutes.
- Add the spinach purée, salt and freshly ground peppercorns, and cook for another five minutes or till the rice is tender. Adjust seasoning.
- Serve hot, garnished with grated Parmesan cheese.

Spinach Soup

1 kilogram spinach, roughly chopped

1 medium onion, chopped

1 tablespoon oil

1 bay leaf

6-8 black peppercorns

5 garlic cloves, chopped

3 cups Vegetable Stock (page 94) or water

½ teaspoon cumin powder

Salt to taste

½ teaspoon white pepper powder

1 cup milk

- Heat the oil in a non-stick pan; add the bay leaf, peppercorns and chopped garlic. Stir-fry for half a minute.
- Add the chopped onion and cook, stirring continuously until the onion turns soft and translucent.

- Add the chopped spinach and continue to cook for three to four minutes. Cool the mixture.
- Remove the bay leaf and purée the spinach mixture to a fine consistency in a blender.
- Bring the vegetable stock or water to a boil; add the spinach purée, cumin powder, salt and white pepper powder to taste. Mix well, lower the heat and simmer for a few minutes.
- Stir in the milk and simmer for two minutes. Serve hot.

Spinach And Tofu Soup

250 grams spinach, roughly shredded

100 grams bean curd (tofu)

1 teaspoon oil

½ inch ginger, chopped

2 garlic cloves, chopped

3 cups Vegetable Stock (page 94)

1 tablespoon light soy sauce

Salt to taste

Black pepper powder to taste

- Cut the tofu into one-fourth inch thick slices and then into one-inch triangles.
- In a non-stick wok or frying pan, heat the oil on high heat and sauté chopped ginger and garlic.
- Add the vegetable stock and bring to a boil.

- Add the tofu and light soy sauce, and bring to a boil; lower the heat and simmer for about two minutes.
- Add the shredded spinach leaves and simmer for a minute, stirring gently. Remove the scum to clarify the soup.
- Add the salt and pepper powder to taste, and serve hot.

Spinach and Tofu Soup

Toasted Almond Soup

20-25 almonds

1 medium carrot, chopped

1 medium onion, chopped

1½ tablespoons butter

5-6 cloves

1 cup White Sauce (page 94)

2 cups milk or water

½ cup fresh cream

Salt to taste

¼ teaspoon white pepper powder

- Soak the almonds in warm water for half an hour and peel. Slice half the almonds into fine slivers and toast in an oven or on non-stick *tawa* until golden brown, and set aside for garnishing.

- Heat the butter in a non-stick pan; add the cloves, carrot and onion, and sauté till the onion turns translucent. Add the remaining almonds. Stir-fry for few minutes.

- Add one cup of water, bring to a boil and cook for five minutes.
- Strain and purée the vegetables and almonds. Transfer to a non-stick pan.
- Dilute the white sauce with the milk and stir into the purée. Place the mixture on heat and bring to a boil. Lower the heat; add the cream and simmer for five minutes. Adjust seasoning with salt and white pepper powder.
- Garnish the soup with the sliced toasted almonds and serve hot.

Tomato And Carrot Soup

8 medium tomatoes, roughly chopped

2 medium carrots, roughly chopped

1 medium potato, roughly chopped

1 medium onion, sliced

4 garlic cloves, crushed

2 cups Vegetable Stock (page 94) or water

1 bay leaf

4-6 black peppercorns

4-6 fresh mint leaves

Salt to taste

2 slices brown bread

- Toast the bread slices in a toaster and cut toasted slices with a sharp knife into small square pieces.
- Alternatively, cut the bread slices into small pieces and dry-roast in a non-stick pan, tossing continuously, till crisp.

- Pressure-cook all the vegetables including onion and garlic along with one cup of vegetable stock or water, bay leaf, peppercorns, mint leaves and salt till completely cooked.

- Cool the cooked mixture. Remove the bay leaf and purée the mixture in a blender

- Transfer the puréed vegetables to a non-stick pan and place it back on heat. Add the remaining vegetable stock or water and adjust salt.

- Simmer for five minutes and serve with toasted brown bread croûtons.

Sweetcorn Vegetable Soup

¼ cup sweetcorn kernels

150 grams cream-style sweetcorn

¼ small cabbage, chopped

¼ medium carrot, diced

1 tablespoon oil

4 cups Vegetable Stock (page 94)

Salt to taste

¼ teaspoon white pepper powder

½ tablespoon sugar

1½ tablespoons cornflour

1 spring onion green stalk, chopped

- Heat the oil in a non-stick wok or pan; add the corn kernels, cabbage and carrot, and stir-fry for a couple of minutes. Stir in the vegetable stock and bring to a boil.

- Mix in the cream-style corn and continue cooking for two to three minutes, or until well mixed.

Sweetcorn Vegetable Soup

- Add the salt, white pepper powder and sugar. Mix the cornflour with one-fourth cup of water and stir into the mixture. Cook, stirring continuously, on high heat for one minute, or until the soup thickens.

- Serve piping hot, garnished with the spring onion greens.

Tomato And Coriander Soup

12 medium-sized ripe red tomatoes, roughly chopped

2 tablespoons fresh coriander, chopped

2 tablespoons olive oil

1 bay leaf

1 medium onion, roughly chopped

12 garlic cloves, roughly chopped

Salt to taste

8 black peppercorns, freshly crushed

1 tablespoon cornflour

2 tablespoons fresh cream

- Heat the olive oil in a deep non-stick pan. Add the bay leaf, onion and garlic, and sauté till well browned to give a burnt flavour.

- Add the tomatoes and stir. Add the salt and crushed black peppercorns, and mix. Stir in one and a half cups of water and cook for three to four minutes.

- Discard the bay leaf. Add the chopped coriander and mix. Crush the mixture with a hand blender while the mixture is cooking.

- Mix the cornflour with two tablespoons of water and add to the soup. Mix and adjust salt. Simmer for two minutes.

- Pour fresh cream in a serving bowl and pour the soup over the cream. Garnish with a small sprig of coriander and serve piping hot.

Cream Of Broccoli And Burnt Garlic Soup

1 medium head of broccoli, separated into small florets

10-12 garlic cloves, halved horizontally

2 teaspoons olive oil

1 medium onion, chopped

1 bay leaf

1 medium potato, finely chopped

3 cups Vegetable Stock (page 94)

Salt to taste

Black pepper powder to taste

1 cup milk

1 small red capsicum, chopped

- Heat one teaspoon of olive oil in a non-stick pan; add the garlic and sauté till the garlic is burnt. Add the onion and bay leaf, and continue to sauté for a minute.

- Add the potato, vegetable stock, salt and pepper powder. When the mixture comes to a boil, cover and cook till the potatoes are tender. Remove the bay leaf and add the broccoli florets.

- Stir and bring to a boil again. Lower the heat and simmer for two minutes.
- Using a hand blender, blend the mixture to a smooth purée. Alternatively, purée the mixture in a blender till smooth.
- Add the milk to the purée and bring it to a boil.
- Heat the remaining olive oil in another non-stick pan; add the red capsicum and sauté for a minute.
- Serve the soup piping hot in individual soup bowls, garnished with the red capsicum.

Cream of Broccoli and Burnt Garlic Soup

Vegetable Soup With Kidney Beans

1 medium carrot, cut into ¼-inch pieces

10-15 French beans, chopped

½ cup fresh button mushrooms, cut into small pieces

1 medium capsicum, cut into ¼-inch pieces

1 medium cucumber, seeded and cut into ¼-inch pieces

⅓ cup red kidney beans

1 medium onion, chopped

4 garlic cloves, chopped

2 medium tomatoes, puréed

3 cups Vegetable Stock (page 94) or water

Salt to taste

½ teaspoon red chilli powder

Fresh chopped coriander, for garnishing

- Soak the kidney beans in sufficient water overnight. Pressure-cook the beans along with the onion and garlic until soft. Drain and reserve the cooking liquid. Mash the kidney beans lightly.

- In a non-stick pan, mix together the mashed kidney beans and the cooking liquid. Stir in the puréed tomatoes and bring to a boil.

- Add the carrot, French beans and vegetable stock, and cook on low heat till the carrot is cooked.

- Stir in the mushrooms, salt, chilli powder and capsicum. Simmer for five minutes and add the cucumber.

- Serve hot, garnished with chopped coriander.

Cyprus Tomato Soup

7-8 medium-sized ripe tomatoes, roughly chopped

½ cup small pasta shells

1 tablespoon olive oil

1 medium onion. finely chopped

5-6 garlic cloves, finely chopped

1 two-inch celery stalk, finely chopped

1 bay leaf

2 cups Vegetable Stock (page 94)

Salt to taste

½ teaspoon black pepper powder

1 tablespoon chopped fresh parsley

- Heat the olive oil in a non-stick pan; add the onion, garlic, celery, and bay leaf, and sauté for a few minutes.

- Add the chopped tomatoes and one cup of vegetable stock and stir. Cook on high heat till it comes to a boil.

- Lower the heat, cover and simmer for fifteen to twenty minutes, stirring occasionally, until the tomatoes are very soft. Strain and reserve the stock.

- Cool the cooked tomatoes and purée them in a blender. Stir in the reserved stock.

- Heat the puréed tomato mixture in a non-stick pan; add the remaining vegetable stock and bring it to a boil.

- Add the pasta, cover and simmer till the pasta is cooked. Add salt and pepper.

- Garnish with chopped parsley and serve hot.

Clear Lemon And Coriander Soup

- 2¾ teaspoons lemon juice
- ½ teaspoon grated lemon rind
- 3 tablespoons chopped fresh coriander
- 1 medium carrot, cut into ½-inch pieces
- 2-3 pieces of baby corn, cut into ½-inch pieces
- ¼ small head of broccoli, separated into florets
- 1 tablespoon oil
- 1 spring onion, chopped
- 2 garlic cloves, finely chopped
- ¼ small Chinese cabbage, cut into ½-inch pieces
- 2-3 fresh button mushrooms, sliced
- 4 cups Vegetable Stock (page 94)
- Salt to taste
- 4-5 black peppercorns, freshly crushed
- ¼ teaspoon MSG (optional)

Clear Lemon and Coriander Soup

- Blanch the carrot, baby corn and broccoli in boiling water for one minute. Drain, refresh in cold water and set aside.

- Heat the oil in a non-stick wok; add the spring onion and garlic, and sauté on medium heat for half a minute.

- Add the Chinese cabbage and mushrooms, and stir-fry on high heat for two minutes. Stir in the vegetable stock and bring to a boil.

- Add the blanched vegetables and cook on high heat for one minute. Stir in the salt, crushed peppercorns, lemon rind and MSG, and continue cooking for another minute.

- Add the lemon juice and the chopped coriander. Stir to mix and serve hot.

Broccoli And Toasted Almond Soup

400 grams broccoli, separated into small florets

10-12 almonds, roasted and slivered

Salt to taste

4 cups Vegetable Stock (page 94), or water

1 medium onion, roughly chopped

4 garlic cloves, roughly chopped

1 two-inch celery stalk, chopped

1 cup milk

White pepper powder to taste

- Soak the broccoli in salted water for ten to fifteen minutes; drain.
- In a deep non-stick pan, bring the vegetable stock, onion, garlic and celery to a boil.
- Add the broccoli florets and continue to cook, uncovered, for five to seven minutes, or till the broccoli is tender.

- Remove from heat, cool and purée the vegetables in a blender.
- Pour the purée back into the pan and stir in the milk; place on heat and bring the mixture to a boil.
- Season with salt and white pepper powder. Stir in the toasted almond slivers and serve hot.

Mushroom, Celery And Garlic Soup

40 fresh button mushrooms, chopped
4 celery stalks, chopped
3 garlic cloves chopped
2 teaspoons oil
4 cups Vegetable Stock (page 94)
2 tablespoons Worcestershire sauce
1 teaspoon grated nutmeg
Salt to taste
Black pepper powder to taste
2 tablespoons fresh cream
Celery leaves, to garnish

- Heat the oil in a non-stick pan. Add the mushrooms, celery and garlic, and sauté for two to three minutes.
- Add half the stock and cook for two to three minutes. Process the vegetables in a blender till smooth.

- Pour the blended mixture into a deep non-stick pan and add the remaining stock, Worcestershire sauce and grated nutmeg.
- Bring to a boil and season the soup with salt and pepper powder. Stir in the cream.
- Serve hot, garnished with the celery leaves.

Mushroom, Celery and Garlic Soup

Potato And Onion Soup

4 medium potatoes, cut into cubes

2 medium onions, chopped

4 tablespoons olive oil

3-4 garlic cloves, chopped

3-4 leeks, sliced

2 tablespoons hazelnuts

1 bay leaf

5-6 black peppercorns

Salt to taste

2 spring onion green stalks, chopped

3-4 basil leaves

2 cups milk

1 large fresh red chilli, chopped

- Heat two tablespoons of olive oil in a non-sick pan; add the onions and sauté for a minute. Add the garlic and leeks, and continue to sauté till soft.

- Add the potato cubes and hazelnuts, and continue to sauté for two to three minutes.

- Add the bay leaf, peppercorns, salt and three cups of water, and cook. Add the spring onion greens and cook till the potatoes are very soft. Add the basil leaves and mix, and cook for a minute.

- Remove the bay leaf and strain the soup. Cool the potato mixture and purée in a blender.

- Mix the purée with the strained stock and adjust salt. Bring the mixture to a boil.

- Add the milk, mix and bring again to a boil.

- Heat the remaining olive oil in another non-stick pan; add the chopped red chillies and sauté for a minute.

- Pour the soup into individual soup bowls, garnish with the sautéed red chillies along with the oil and serve hot.

Dal Aur Gajar Shorba

½ cup split pigeon peas

2 tablespoons split green gram with skin

2 medium carrots

2-3 whole dried red chillies

6-8 black peppercorns

1 teaspoon cumin seeds

1 teaspoon coriander seeds

4-5 garlic cloves

2 green chillies, slit

Salt to taste

2 tablespoons fresh coriander, chopped

- Soak the split pigeon peas in two cups of water and the split green gram with the skin in half a cup of water, separately, for half an hour. Drain.

- Cut one carrot roughly and grate the other coarsely. Dry-roast the red chillies, peppercorns, cumin seeds and coriander seeds, and grind together to a coarse powder.

- Put the pigeon peas and the green gram in a pressure cooker. Add the roughly cut carrot, garlic and three cups of water, and cook till the lentils are very soft.

- Mash the lentils with a hand blender till smooth. Add one cup of water and green chillies, and bring to a boil. Add the ground spices and salt. Simmer for two minutes.

- Serve, garnished with fresh coriander and grated carrot.

Thai Green Curry Noodle Soup

1½ tablespoons Thai Green Curry Paste (page 94)

200 grams eggless noodles, boiled

2 tablespoons oil

½ small head of broccoli, separated into small florets

½ cup corn kernels

1 medium carrot, cut into diamonds

1 medium red capsicum, cut into ½-inch triangles

4-5 fresh button mushrooms, sliced

2 cups Vegetable Stock (page 94)

Salt to taste

1 teaspoon lemon juice

1cup fresh Coconut Milk (page 93)

½ cup bean sprouts

1 fresh red chilli, diagonally sliced

3-4 fresh basil leaves

Thai Green Curry Noodle Soup

- Heat the oil in a non-stick pan. Add the broccoli, corn, carrot, red capsicum and mushrooms, and sauté for a minute.

- Add the green curry paste and mix well. Add the vegetable stock and salt, and cook till the vegetables are almost tender, and not overcooked.

- Stir in the lemon juice and coconut milk, and heat the soup through.

- Place a ring mould in the centre of soup bowl and pack it with the boiled noodles. Pour the soup into the soup bowl around the ring mould. Sprinkle the bean sprouts.

- Slowly remove the ring mould so as not to disturb the noodles. Sprinkle red chilli over the noodles and place the basil leaves on top.

- Serve immediately.

Garlic Rasam

15-20 garlic cloves, roasted

2 tablespoons split pigeon peas, soaked

1 medium tomato, cubed

2 teaspoons Tamarind Pulp (page 93)

Salt to taste

A pinch of asafoetida

¼ teaspoon turmeric powder

Rasam Powder

1 teaspoon cumin seeds

6-8 black peppercorns

4 dried red chillies

1 tablespoon coriander seeds

1 teaspoon split Bengal gram

Seasoning

½ teaspoon mustard seeds

2 dried red chillies

1 sprig curry leaves

- Boil three cups of water in a deep non-stick pan. Add the split pigeon peas and tomato cubes and cook, covered, till soft. Mash and reserve along with the water.

- For the *rasam* powder, in a non-stick pan, dry-roast the cumin seeds, peppercorns, red chillies, coriander seeds and split Bengal gram till light brown. Cool and pound to a powder.

- Add three cups of water to the tamarind pulp and boil it with the salt, asafoetida, turmeric powder and *masala* powder for five minutes. Add the mashed pigeon peas to the *rasam* and bring it to a boil.

- Lower the heat and simmer for five minutes. Strain and bring to a boil again.

- For the seasoning, dry-roast the mustard seeds, red chillies and curry leaves in a non-stick pan and add it to the boiling *rasam*.
- Cover immediately to trap the flavours. Serve piping hot, garnished with roasted garlic.

Chef's Tip

You can pound the garlic very lightly before adding to the *rasam*, for a stronger flavour. You can also pressure-cook the garlic separately and then add it to the *rasam*. Increase or decrease the quantity of garlic to taste.

Narangi Shorba

1 cup fresh orange juice

3 medium carrots, roughly chopped

500 grams red pumpkin, roughly chopped

1 medium onion, roughly chopped

2 green chillies, roughly chopped

1 teaspoon cumin seeds, roasted and powdered

Salt to taste

½ cup fresh cream

A few sprigs of fresh coriander

- Heat a non-stick pan; add the carrots, pumpkin, onion, green chillies and one cup of water. Cook on medium heat for eight to ten minutes, or till the vegetables are soft. Cool the cooked vegetables slightly and purée in a blender.
- Transfer the purée to a non-stick pan. Add the cumin seed powder, salt and one cup of water to the vegetable purée and bring to a boil. Lower the heat, add the fresh orange juice and simmer for two to three minutes.
- Stir in the fresh cream and serve hot, garnished with sprigs of fresh coriander.

Annexure

- *Chilli Oil*

  Cook 6 tablespoons of chopped dried red chillies in 1 ¼ cups of groundnut oil on low heat for at least ten minutes. When completely cold, stir in 2-3 tablespoons of red chilli powder and 1-2 tablespoons of sesame oil. Cover and leave to stand for at least twelve hours. Strain into a sterilised bottle and store in a cool, dark place.

- *Coconut Milk*

  Process 1 cup grated fresh coconut in a blender with ¼ cup warm water. Pass the ground coconut through a piece of muslin or strainer pressing firmly to extract all the juice, or first milk. Add ¼ cup of warm water to the strained coconut to get the second, thinner milk from the same solids.

- *Tamarind Pulp*

  Soak 75 grams tamarind in 100 ml warm water for 10-15 minutes. Grind to a smooth paste and strain to remove any fibres. Store in an airtight container in the refrigerator.

- ***Thai Green Curry Paste***

  Grind together 10 green chillies, 3 shallots, 9 garlic cloves, 1-inch galangal, 3-inch lemon grass stalk, ¼ teaspoon grated lemon rind, a small bunch of coriander roots, 2 teaspoons coriander seeds, 2 teaspoons cumin seeds and salt to taste to make a fine paste.

- ***Vegetable Stock***

  Peel, wash and chop 1 onion, ½ medium carrot, 2-3 inch celery stalk and 2-3 garlic cloves. Place in a pan with 1 bay leaf, 5-6 peppercorns, 2-3 cloves and 5 cups of water and bring to a boil. Lower heat and simmer for 15 minutes and strain. Cool and store in a refrigerator till further use.

- ***White Sauce***

  To make the white sauce, melt 2 tablespoons butter in a heavy-bottomed pan and stir in 2 tablespoons refined flour. Cook for five to six minutes over low heat till fragrant. Whisk in 2 cups milk till smooth. Cook for four to five minutes, stirring continuously, till the sauce thickens. Add salt to taste and ½ teaspoon white pepper powder and mix well. Strain the sauce. Makes 2 cups.

Variations:

Cream sauce: Add ¼ cup of cream and 2 tablespoons of melted butter to the white sauce.

Parsley sauce: Add 1 tablespoon of chopped parsley to the cream sauce.

Glossary

ENGLISH	HINDI
Almonds	Badam
Bay leaf	Tej patta
Beetroot	Chukander
Black-eyed beans	Chowli
Broccoli	Hara gobhi
Cabbage	Pattagobhi
Capsicum	Shimla mirch
Carrots	Gajar
Cauliflower	Phoolgobhi
Celery	Ajmoda
Cloves	laung
Coriander seeds	Dhania
Cottage cheese	Paneer
Cream	Malai
Cumin seeds	Jeera
Green gram, split, with skin	Chilkewali moong dal
Lettuce leaves	Salad ke patte
Mushroom	Khumb
Olives	Jaitun
Orange	Narangi
Pigeon peas, split	Toovar/Arhar dal
Red kidney beans	Rajma
Sesame seeds	Til
Spinach	Palak
Spring onions	Hare pyaaz
Vermicelli	Sevian
Wholewheat flour	Atta